D1116368

Charles Proteus Steinmetz

Wizard of Electricity

SCIENCE STORY LIBRARY

Charles Proteus Steinmetz
Wizard of Electricity

BY ERICK BERRY

ILLUSTRATED BY JOHN MARTINEZ

The Macmillan Company, New York
Collier-Macmillan Limited, London

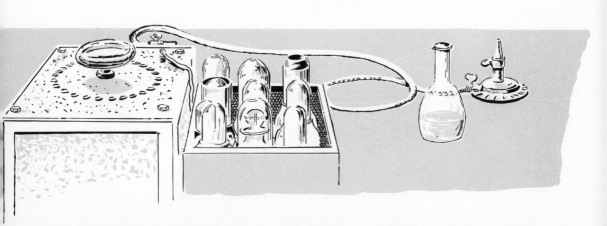

Charles Proteus Steinmetz

Wizard of Electricity

In the small city of Breslau, Germany, there was born, in 1865, a boy named Karl August Rudolf Steinmetz. He was a cripple. As a boy he was small for his age, and he had a humped back and a large head. But he had very bright eyes that looked out from under a thatch of black hair, and in that large head was one of the finest mathematical minds the world has ever known.

In those days, the power of electricity had been discovered, but it had not yet been put to work. People had no electric lights, no electric stoves, and no electric motors to run refrigerators, operate pumps, or start cars. Karl Steinmetz would do much to change all that.

Karl lived with his father and his grandmother, both of whom were very fond of him and did all they could to help him with his studies. When he was seventeen

years old he entered Breslau University. He usually stood at the top of his class in physics and higher mathematics, and he also found the time to help his fellow students and to join in their parties and jokes.

He was elected to the important University Mathematics Society—a great honor indeed. In this society each member had a nickname. Karl expected that his nickname would make fun of him. But, to his surprise, the members called him "Proteus." When he asked a friend, "Why did you call me Proteus?" the friend laughed and said, "You are like Proteus, the Roman god who was able to take on so many faces and do so many things." Karl was proud of his new name.

Karl's very active brain sometimes got him into trouble. At that time Germany was ruled by the harsh Chancellor Prince Otto von Bismarck. Bismarck did not believe that everyone should have the vote. The students at the university published a small newspaper criticizing the government. The editor of the paper, a friend of Karl's, was sent to prison because of what he had written.

Karl agreed to publish the paper for him. This was a dangerous thing to do. Karl was a favorite of the professors, and one of them warned him. "The police are watching you," he said. "You had better leave the country."

Karl knew it would be dangerous for his father to help him escape, so early one morning he woke his father and said, "Today I am going to the country with a friend." What he really wanted to say was "Goodbye."

His father said sleepily, "Well, have a nice holiday!" They never saw each other again.

Karl went directly to the railroad station and bought a round-trip ticket to a town near the Austrian border. If the police were watching him, they would think he planned to return. At the border he bought another round-trip ticket to Switzerland.

In Zurich, Switzerland, Karl was safe, but he had no money, no change of clothes, and no job. But he had

his fine mind. He began to write scientific articles for the papers. He wanted to finish his studies at the famous Polytechnique school, but because he had no official papers from Germany the school would not accept him.

The average young man would have become discouraged by so much trouble. But when things looked dark, Karl always had an amazing stroke of luck. In Zurich he met the editor of a newspaper for which he had written when he was in Breslau. The editor wanted more articles from Karl, and he arranged to have Karl enter the Polytechnique and continue his studies. Karl earned a little by teaching other students.

Then came another stroke of luck: he made friends with a Danish student, Oscar Asmussen. The young men decided to room together. Oscar had a rich uncle in California who sent him an allowance each month. Oscar had fallen in love with a Swiss girl and wanted to marry her.

Young Asmussen talked a lot about America, its freedom from secret police, and how simple it was to earn a living there. Karl thought it all sounded too good to be true, and he was sure he would never be able to get to America. One day Oscar received a cable from his uncle ordering him to break his engagement to the

Swiss girl and to leave at once for America. To make sure he would do this, his uncle had stopped Oscar's allowance and had sent him a first-class steamship ticket.

Oscar was very unhappy. "What shall I do?" he asked Karl.

"You can obey your uncle and marry the girl too," Karl pointed out. "Go to America and get a job. Then send for your fiancée."

Oscar was delighted at the idea. "I will take you with me," he said. "I'll exchange my first-class ticket for two steerage tickets so we can go together."

At first this seemed more than Karl could accept

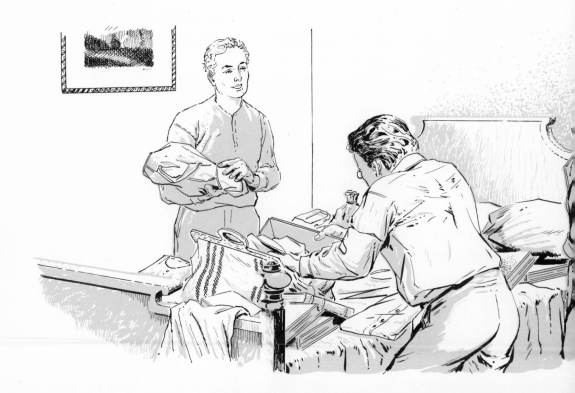

from a friend, but Oscar persuaded him and went to exchange the ticket. While Karl was packing his few belongings he heard footsteps on the stairs and then a knock at his door. A stranger entered.

"My name is Uppencorn," said the man. "I am a publisher. I have read your scientific articles and would like to order some writing from you."

When Karl explained that he would soon be leaving for America, the editor thought quickly. "Perhaps in America you would act as foreign correspondent for my paper. I will also give you a letter to a young scientist, Rudolf Eickemeyer, a well-known American inventor."

Again Karl's good luck was working for him.

The trip across the Atlantic was very rough and uncomfortable. Karl spent much of the voyage in his bunk with a bad cold. But he tried to learn as much English as he could in the short time on the ocean.

When the ship docked in New York it seemed as though Karl's luck had changed. America wanted only able-bodied workers, not sickly, poorly dressed ones. Besides, Karl could show no money. The officer in charge said, "You cannot enter the United States with no money. You will have to return on this ship."

Suddenly Oscar came running. "Officer," he said, "I have this young man's money. He gave it to me for safekeeping."

For a while the two young men lived with Oscar's relatives in New York. Karl went to New Jersey to look for work with the Edison Company, for he was an admirer of Thomas Edison, the great inventor. Surely there would be a place for him in the Edison plant. But the Chief Engineer would not even talk to Karl. When he saw that Karl looked shabby, and was a cripple, he turned him away. Karl went back to New York very much discouraged.

He then decided to use his letter of introduction to Rudolf Eickemeyer. Eickemeyer's office was in Yonkers,

New York, where he manufactured machinery for making hats. Karl's letter admitted him immediately to the head office. When Eickemeyer invited him to sit down, Karl began to stammer in his broken English about his work in Switzerland.

"Don't you speak German?" said Eickemeyer in German. When Karl began to talk in his own tongue the two men found they could exchange ideas immediately. They talked more than two hours. When Karl left, he had the promise of a job. The following week

he started designing machinery for the Eickemeyer factory.

The pay was not good even for those days, and the hours were long. For twelve dollars a week, young Steinmetz had to rise at five o'clock in the morning in order to make the long trip to Yonkers, and he was never back home until very late.

Now that he was sure of his job, Karl wanted to become a citizen of the country where he had found work and freedom. He went to the Federal Building in New York and applied for naturalization papers. He was twenty-three years old. It would take some time before he could become a full citizen, but at least he had made a start.

Eickemeyer had a laboratory next to his factory. Here he designed his inventions. He soon made Karl his assistant in the laboratory and put him in charge of the whole plant. Karl was well liked by the men who worked under him. The little man who spoke guttural English was surprisingly popular. He was never too busy to help others, just as he had helped his fellow students at the university in Germany.

The working day at the factory was a full twelve hours, and Karl was usually the first to arrive. When his friend Oscar left for California, Karl went to board with a fellow worker who lived near the factory. This gave him more time to continue his studies and his experiments in the laboratory.

Eickemeyer asked Karl to design a new kind of electric motor. Many people had tried to do this but without success. Karl started to read everything that had been printed about electricity. Some of the books were in French and German, some in Latin, some in Greek. But none of them told him anything about *hysteresis*, which means "delay."

There are two kinds of electric motors and generators. One uses direct current, which is like water being pumped steadily through a pipe. The other uses alternating current, which is like water being pumped backward and forward through a pipe. When a generator makes alternating current, or when the motor uses it, there is a very slight pause when the current stops going in one direction and starts going in the other. This pause is called "hysteresis." Hysteresis takes only the smallest fraction of a second, but it somehow causes motors and generators to become too hot. Karl knew that if he wanted to design better motors and generators, he must cut down this delay.

Karl was a brilliant mathematician. He filled many notebooks with figures from his own and other inven-

tors' experiments. Now he tried to find from these figures what had happened in these experiments.

Karl had become a member of the American Institute
of Electrical Engineers and of the New York Mathematical Society. At the meetings of these societies he

usually listened and learned but did not speak. But in 1889, at a lecture called "The Armature Reaction of Alternators," he found that another member of the society had been studying hysteresis. Karl stood up in the meeting and began to describe what he had discovered. He then wrote a paper for the society explaining his ideas more fully. In 1891, when he published this paper, called "The Law of Hysteresis," he almost immediately became world-famous. This was only two

and a half years after the young genius's arrival in America.

Now that Karl had discovered *why* alternating current behaved as it did, he knew *how* to use it. He almost always proceeded that way, from mathematics to engineering, from *why* to *how*. The important result was that better alternating-current generators and motors could now be made and could be used for many purposes.

One day when receiving his weekly pay envelope, Karl signed his long name, Karl August Rudolf Steinmetz. The man in line behind him said, "That's a long German name for an American." Karl wanted very much to be an American, so he decided to change his name. Karl, of course, is Charles in English. But Americans always had a middle name. What should he choose? He remembered his old nickname, Proteus, the one the Mathematics Society had given him at the university. He decided to become Charles Proteus Steinmetz, and under that name he took out his citizenship papers.

Charles was very happy. He was an American now, and he enjoyed his job. When Eickemeyer told him that the big General Electric Company was buying his plant and would move it to Lynn, Massachusetts, Charles said he did not intend to move with it. He preferred to stay where he was.

Eickemeyer tried to persuade him, but he could not. Finally he used his strongest argument: "If you work for General Electric, my boy," he said, "you will have a wonderful laboratory and all kinds of equipment for your experiments. You would be foolish to turn down so good an offer."

This, of course, was just the right thing to say. Charles accepted, and in 1893 he went to the new plant in Lynn. He stayed with General Electric the rest of his life.

Charles hated leaving his friends in Yonkers. In Lynn he rented a shabby little room in a poor part of town, and the next Monday he reported for work. He had felt lonely and forlorn in this strange town and was therefore pleasantly surprised by a warm welcome at the new laboratory. Almost everyone knew of his important work with electricity and hysteresis. He was told that anything he wanted for his work would be given to him. This was good news, indeed. Perhaps the move to Lynn wasn't going to be so bad as he had feared.

Actually, Charles Steinmetz had created this job for himself without realizing it. His discovery of how to make alternating motors and generators had led to a sudden growth in the electrical industry. But this growth was now slowing down because nobody knew how to make the alternating current safe to use in houses. This new current had to be very powerful in order to travel long distances over wires, but it also had to be changed and made weaker to be used in the home. Even Edison, the great American inventor, said that it "could never be tamed."

The device for taming it is called a "transformer." You can see a transformer today: it is the round black box perched on the electric pole near your house. The transformer had been invented by an American engineer, William Stanley, but it was not very successful. So the first assignment General Electric gave Charles was to "make us a better transformer."

Charles had seen the need for this and had been working on the problem by himself for three years. The main difficulty was that alternating current could not be measured with a simple instrument, as could direct current. In fact, the force pulled and pushed backward and forward so rapidly that it did not seem to move at all.

Charles had been working in Lynn for some weeks when one of his friends said, "You look ill, Charles. You are getting thinner and thinner. It looks as though you are not eating enough."

The young man did not want to talk about his troubles, but finally he admitted that since he had joined the new firm he had not been paid. He had had to live very cheaply, and the only way he could do that was to go without meals. This was immediately reported to the head of the firm, and it was discovered that Charles's name had never been put on the payroll. The company at once paid him all that was due him, and for the first time since coming to Lynn he had a fine meal.

Charles and his assistants were making hundreds of experiments in the laboratory. Charles continued to fill many notebooks with figures in a sort of shorthand he had invented. Finally he was pleased to announce that he had found a way to measure the current by simple algebra. He was asked to read a paper on this discovery before the International Electrical Congress in Chicago.

The paper may have seemed simple to Charles, but his explanation was far over the heads of most of the engineers in his audience. When he had been reading awhile, he looked up and saw that there were only a few persons left in the hall to listen to him. He apologized, saying, "I am sorry. I am still only halfway through my introduction." Later he published the whole "paper," which he called *The General Number*. The simple algebraic equation had become a huge manuscript, published in three thick volumes. Now the engineers at General Electric were able to design transformers that would make electricity safe to use in houses everywhere. This was Charles Steinmetz's greatest contribution to America, the land he loved.

Then General Electric transferred Charles to Schenectady, New York, on the Mohawk River. This move did not worry him as had the move to Lynn. He found

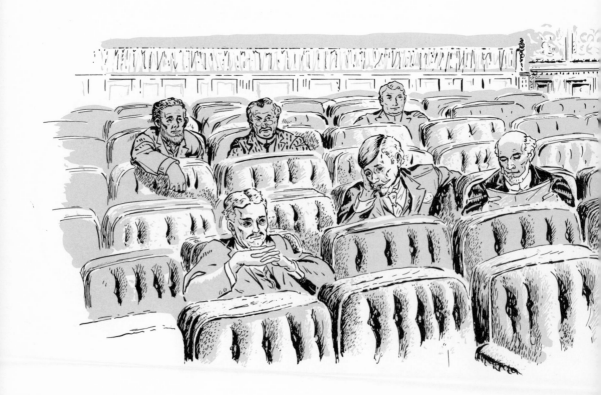

the old Dutch town rather like his home town of Breslau, Germany, and knew he would be content there.

Still, he hated to live alone. He always liked having
people around him. In the new laboratory he found a
young engineer named Ernst Berg and suggested that
they rent a house together. Charles said he would be
glad to do all the cooking. He had studied chemistry in

Germany and thought he was a good cook. Unfortunately no one agreed with him.

In the Schenectady laboratory Charles was already well known. Many of the engineers had talked or worked with him in Lynn. Soon the townspeople began to know him too. Steinmetz, traveling back and forth to work on his bicycle, waved to acquaintances on the sidewalk, stopped to talk with the children and give them candy and even to join in their play. He was never too busy for children.

One of Charles's first duties at the Schenectady plant was to teach the new theory of General Number and alternating current to the other engineers. Often his explanations were too difficult for them to understand, but he was always patient and would explain again and again. Others came to him with their most difficult mathematical problems. Sometimes he would solve these problems on paper, but often he could work them out in his head and give the answers.

Charles and Ernst turned the coach house of their big old house into a laboratory. This made room in the main house for many visitors, who often stayed overnight and slept on one of the camp beds Charles had set up. Of course they had to put up with his experiments in cooking.

Besides his visitors from Union College, where he had been teaching, Charles had other guests—permanent ones. These were his many animals. People soon learned about his fondness for animals and brought him mice, tropical fish, a raccoon, and other creatures. He was especially fond of two crows named Mary and John, who had come to him as fledglings. They were very tame and were allowed to fly about in the house and even outdoors. But they were terrible thieves. In the early morning they would fly through a neighbor's open window and return to Charles with a bit of bright jewelry, a button, or anything small and shiny. To discover the owner of the property, Charles had to wait till some angry neighbor came to complain.

Each evening when he returned from work John and

24

Mary would swoop down from a tree to light on the handlebars of his bicycle and ride to the coach house. Charles claimed that he had learned crow language and could talk to them.

One of the puzzling things about Charles Steinmetz was his enormous ability to work and play. He would return from a full day at the General Electric laboratory and go straight to his own laboratory in the coach house. Or he would welcome a small boy with a sick animal or a broken toy, listen to his troubles, and, when the toy was mended, spend hours playing with it. He enjoyed both work and play. One thing that never interested Charles was himself. When important visitors from abroad came to talk to him about his wonderful discoveries in electricity they wore tall silk hats and tailcoats. But they were greeted by the electrical wizard in comfortable shabby old pants and an undershirt.

He claimed that such visitors wanted to know not Charles Steinmetz but some algebraic equations. And an equation could not wear a collar and tie.

The General Electric Company loaned Charles to Union College to lecture to future electrical engineers. His talks were very popular, and he was so much liked by the students that they voted him a member of the Phi Gamma Delta fraternity, an honor of which he was very proud.

All his hours at the laboratory and in his lectures were not enough to weary this remarkable man. Out of his weekend canoe trips on the Mohawk River had grown another interest. He bought a site on the river-bank and had a neighboring farmer build a small wooden camp there. Over many years the camp grew

and grew, since visiting engineers and students came there by canoe or bicycle. They did their own cooking and sat around the campfire at night to discuss electrical problems with their host.

Charles was now thinking and experimenting along a new line. His first great discovery had been producing alternating current efficiently. His second discovery had been taming this current by transformers. He was concerned with finding out how high-voltage alternating current could be carried along electric wires from the generating plant to points where it was needed. So much power seemed to leak out along the way. Many of his experiments with this untamed high-voltage current were carried out in the coach-house laboratory.

Little was known about this new force. It was like playing with dynamite, and accidents seemed bound to happen. An accident did wreck the laboratory, but the cause was nothing more than a wire that had been allowed to become red hot. This set fire to the place. The fire department saved the main house, but all of Charles's papers about his experiments were burned.

The landlord was very angry. So was Charles. The landlord asserted that he had lost valuable property and wanted Charles to pay for his loss. Charles claimed that his papers were worth more than the old coach house. Finally General Electric came to the rescue and agreed to pay the landlord.

This quarrel convinced Charles that he should build his own house. General Electric owned a tract of land that was being divided into plots to be sold to employees. Charles chose a site on Wendell Avenue on a slope with a fine view, and in the swamp at the bottom of the hill he saw he could build a water garden for his pet alligator. When the house was finished he planned to have a conservatory for the orchids and cacti he enjoyed raising.

The General Electric Company built him a fine new laboratory, so fine that when it was completed Charles set up his camp bed and slept there. Meanwhile no one lived in the house. Ernst Berg had left to be married, and the big brick house was very lonely. Charles had only his animals for company—two parrots, woodchucks, raccoons, rabbits, mice, turtles, and of course that alligator.

One evening while Charles was talking to his parrots two young men came to call. One was a friend from the General Electric laboratory, the other an engineer from the Lynn plant. The stranger was Roy Hayden, who had been experimenting with street lighting.

Charles put the two parrots back on their perches and asked the young men to stay. Roy Hayden proved to be so well informed on electrical matters that they talked for hours. When he left, Charles invited him to return soon and often. Roy Hayden became a regular visitor to the laboratory and often helped Charles with his work, remaining to spend the night there. Charles became very fond of Roy and adopted him legally. Now he had a son of whom he could be proud and whose work interests he shared. It was through Roy that Charles became interested in street lighting with electricity.

First Steinmetz worked on a mercury lamp. Liquid mercury was heated in a tube, and when the current passed through its vapor it gave a very bright light. But it was more like moonlight than sunlight, because

the mercury tube gave out no red rays. People didn't like the light, for it made everyone look green. Charles was not interested in what it did to ladies' complexions, but when a row of these lights was set up outside his house he was disappointed. They drained his flowers of color, so that they looked green and cold. He soon lost interest in this experiment, but the mercury light is still used today for certain purposes.

It seemed to Charles that alternating current was the further development in the use of electricity. It would be cheaper to use. But if he couldn't find a way to make lamps run on alternating current, perhaps he could do something to make lamps run more economically on direct current.

Street lights must be very bright, or else many poles and lamps would be needed, and they were expensive.

The brightest light already in use was the arc light. This used two sticks shaped like candles, about half an inch thick and made of highly compressed carbon. When the electricity was turned off, their points touched. When the direct current was turned on, it passed from one tip to the other, making the tips white hot. Then a *solenoid*, which is a kind of magnet, began to draw the two black candles apart, so that incandescent particles of carbon passed through the gap from one carbon rod to the other, giving an extremely bright light. The current also passed through the solenoid, which in turn kept the carbon candles at the right distance apart, and let them close again when the current was switched off.

But the trouble was that the carbon candles burned away. If they were to be used in street lighting, men

would have to go around every day with ladders and climb up to replace those that had grown too short. That costly part of the job was what Steinmetz wanted to correct.

Just as Edison had done with the filament lamp, so did Charles make many experiments to find the right material with which to replace the compressed carbon candles. The best one he found was a pure form of magnetic iron called magnetite. He combined this with a rare metal called titanium. For the positive pole he used a copper rod. The result was a light much brighter than the old carbon rods had given, and the new rods lasted much longer.

Charles wanted these new lights to be shown to the people of Schenectady. He got the directors of the electric company to consent to setting up arc lights with the new magnetite candles along Wendell Avenue in front of his house. A Brush-type direct-current generator was put up on the front lawn, so as to be as near as possible, and Roy took personal charge of this part of the project. On the night that the lights were to be shown for the first time people came from all over the city, along with the directors of the company and most of Charles's friends from General Electric.

The lights flickered on, grew brighter and brighter

still, bathing the whole street in the brightest lights anyone had ever seen. The success of the experiment made the gathering seem like a huge party. Charles moved about among the crowd, smoking his cigar, greeting friends he had not seen for a long time, shaking hands and stopping to talk to the children. He was never so happy as when he was among friends, and the more friends the better. When the evening was over, he declared, "I haven't had such a good time in years. This is the way to get to see the people I like!"

General Electric knew the value of Charles Steinmetz's wonderful mind. They trusted him completely and let him do his work in his own way. Some weeks he spent only a few hours in his office, just enough to answer the more difficult questions that came up. But it did not matter to the company whether he worked for them in his office, in his home laboratory, or even in his canoe on the Mohawk River. He gave them more than two hundred valuable patents and solved many puzzling problems for them that no one else could have answered.

The problems that appealed to him most were those that would make life easier for farmers and others who had to lift heavy loads. Charles had always been physically handicapped. Work with his muscles was for him a great hardship, so he was sorry for people who had to earn their living that way.

Now he had made it possible to produce the more efficient alternating current and to tame it with transformers. What he wanted to do next was to make this electricity as cheap as possible. It would cost more to build a lot of small generating stations than to build a few large ones, so he wanted big, strong stations that would carry the current over long distances.

But if the current were to travel over long distances it must be of high voltage—that is to say, very strong.

This was difficult, because there was such waste along the way. High power produced what is called the *corona* effect. The coronas were rings of light that formed in the air around the wire, and these lost power, just as a leaky pipe loses water.

Charles built apparatus in his laboratory to study this loss of power. It flashed high-voltage current through the air, just like lightning. Man-made lightning leaping across the room, with the newspaper reporters sitting within a few feet of the deadly flashes! No wonder Charles's demonstrations often made the headlines. And such dramatic news helped to interest the public in his purpose, which always served to give the people cheaper and better electric power. None of this came all of a sudden, of course; these experiments with the problems of corona covered the years between 1903 and 1913.

Instead of using coal-burning steam engines to turn the generators, he wanted to use water power wherever this was possible. He was interested too in using the power of the sun and of ocean waves. He wished to study everything that would benefit mankind, this inventor with the wonderful mind that could work faster and for longer hours than that of other people.

Charles Steinmetz never wanted to be rich. He often

told his pupils at Union College that they must be interested in their work first of all, not in making money or becoming famous. He himself lived very simply. He smoked many cigars, but he spent almost nothing on his clothes, his house, or his food. He gave a great deal, secretly, to charity, and of course spent even more on his experiments.

All this time Roy lived with him in the laboratory on Wendell Avenue. Roy called him "Daddy." At Union College the students called him "Steinie," but of course to the world and to other scientists he was Dr. Steinmetz. The newspapers dubbed him "The Wizard of Schenectady."

It was rough bachelor housekeeping for Roy and Charles. They still slept on camp beds in the laboratory and cooked over a single-burner stove. Charles insisted on doing the cooking, and he had many strange ideas about food. For a while he insisted that all foods must be yellow. They had carrots, turnips, corn, and scrambled eggs day after day. Then he switched to steak and potatoes for all three meals.

When Roy became engaged to a Schenectady girl, Charles took great interest in the romance. Then one evening, sitting down to another meal of steak and potatoes, Roy announced, "I am going out to get married." He said it much as he might say, "I am going out to get a square meal."

Roy Hayden did get married almost immediately. The young couple went off on their honeymoon, and when they returned they moved into the bride's house, on the other side of town. But the very evening of their return there was a ring at the doorbell. Charles stood on the doorstep. He had been very lonely without Roy. Of course he was invited in to dinner, and for some weeks he returned every night for the evening meal. In the end it seemed simpler for the Haydens to move into

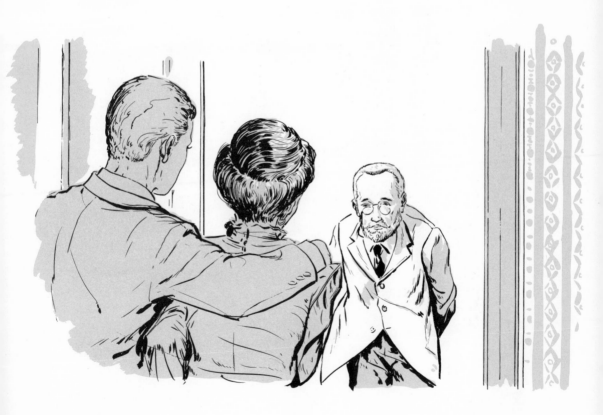

the big, empty Wendell Avenue house and live with Charles. It was a very happy arrangement for all of them.

When the family grew and there were Hayden children, Charles legally adopted them as his grandchildren. The household was busy with toys, children, animals, and much play and laughter. The boy from Breslau had a family of his own now, more money than he needed, a world-wide reputation, and he took great delight in living. No one could ask for more.

When Charles Proteus Steinmetz died he did not leave any great memorial for people to visit. His memorial is all around us. The great city skyscrapers could not have been built if there had been no electric motors to run the elevators. Little, lonely farms on the prairies use electricity for lighting, and big farms on the plains use electric power to milk their cows and lift the hay into the barns. And in our own homes we use washing machines, dishwashers, telephones, radios. We all owe a great debt to the German-born inventor. He took electricity out of the laboratory and tamed it to work for us.

SCIENCE STORY LIBRARY

DATE DUE
